STAYING ABOVE WATER

Global migration in the face of the climate crisis

STAYING ABOVE WATER

Global migration in the face of the climate crisis

Rising Tide North America

2019

First Printing: 2019
ISBN 978-0-359-56642-6

Rising Tide North America
100 S Broad St
PO Box # 22521
Philadelphia, PA 19110

www.RisingTideNorthAmerica.org

Table of Contents

About Rising Tide North America

Rising Tide is an international, all-volunteer, grassroots network of groups and individuals who organize locally, promote community-based solutions to the climate crisis, and take direct action to confront the root causes of climate change.

Rising Tide was born out of the conviction that corporate-friendly "solutions" to climate change will not save us and that most government efforts are half-measures at best. We organize through decentralized local groups that support one another with shared resources, ideas, fundraising, training and collaborations. Our activities include grassroots community organizing, publishing educational materials, organizing creative direct actions and protests, and holding public education events in order to further the struggle for climate justice.

Rising Tide is committed to stopping the extraction of fossil fuels and preventing the construction of new fossil fuel infrastructure. Equally important, we must make a just transition to sustainable livelihoods that foster local autonomy and self-sufficiency.

Rising Tide's tactics are diverse and creative, taking a bottom-up approach to connecting the dots between colonialism, corporate power, climate disruption, social justice, and biocentrism. The systems that are destroying the planet are systems rooted in oppression; combating climate change is therefore not just a matter of carbon emissions, but of confronting the institutions that destroy communities, cultures and the Earth.

Our Story

Rising Tide was formed in the Netherlands in 2000 by environmental and social justice activists attending the UN Conference of the Parties climate talks. Rising Tide now spans four continents, with activists in North and South America, the UK, Ecuador, and Australia.

Rising Tide's North American network was founded in the spring of 2006. Many of Rising Tide's original members met during the original Mountain Justice Summer, inspired by the movement's lack of distinction between human rights and environmental concerns, as well as at Earth First! gatherings.

From the beginning Rising Tide has worked to create a network that prioritizes local grassroots organizing yet remains firmly engaged in international social movements; which promotes solidarity and collaboration with impacted communities and local social justice struggles; which challenges corporate-friendly "solutions" to climate change; and which organizes with a horizontal, anti-oppressive framework that promotes social justice as inextricably linked to biocentrism and environmentalism.

Rising Tide North America now has local contacts in more than 50 cities through Mexico, the United States, and Canada.

Climate Justice

Climate change demands that we ask what kind of world we want to live in. Climate justice and is as much a social issue as an environmental one. Everywhere in the world, low-income, politically marginalized communities— historically those least responsible for CO2 emissions—are also those hardest hit by climate change and every aspect of the energy industry, from toxic pollution to resource wars.

We aim to support communities in making a "just transition," in which social and ecological needs are prioritized in the shift to a low-carbon society. This means opposing policies that cause collateral damage to communities or strengthen existing inequalities. Real solutions to climate chaos are local in nature and come from communities themselves, not from the institutions that got us into this mess.

Climate justice is more than just a goal; it's a practice in the movement against climate chaos. No effort to create a livable future will succeed without the empowerment of marginalized communities and the dismantling of the systems of oppression that keep us divided.

Staying Above Water

More than 30 years ago leading scientists from NASA began warning policymakers that global temperatures were warming as a result of the emissions of carbon and other greenhouse gasses. By the early 1990s, there was a broad and growing consensus within the global scientific community that human emissions of greenhouse gasses were causing significant changes to the global climate.

In the following decades, fossil fuel companies and corporate interests would continue to deny the mounting evidence and even the policymakers who recognized the potentially devastating impacts of global climate change would fail to take decisive action to curb the emissions of greenhouse gasses. At the same time, super storms like hurricanes Katrina and Sandy and Typhoon Haiyan would devastate entire regions, killing thousands and causing hundreds of billions of dollars in damages, providing dramatic examples of the gravity of the risks caused by climate change. Slower onset consequences including multi-year droughts in Somalia, the Sudan and Syria would destabilize entire regions fueling civil conflicts that displaced millions.

After decades of inaction and neglect, the climate crisis is here. Already the rapid warming of the earth is causing changes in weather patterns, increases in both the frequency and occurrence of extreme weather events, sea level rise, floods, droughts, wildfires, and increasing desertification of farmlands [1].

Together, all of these environmental changes are contributing to localized food shortages and conflict over increasingly scarce resources. Around the world, people are being forced to adapt to the changing environment, fortifying homes to withstand superstorms, changing crop patterns and seeking new sources of food and water. As the effects of catastrophic climate change continue to emerge, it is clear that some of the places that people are currently living will become uninhabitable and others will not be able to support current population levels. In the face of the climate crisis, tens of millions of people will likely use migration as a strategy for adapting to climate change, seeking shelter and sustenance in other parts of the world.[2]

A worst-case scenario for climate-change induced migration could involve entire communities rapidly forced from their homelands by flooding or other severe weather events. But climate-induced migration does not necessarily mean the wholesale abandonment of people's historic homelands. Instead, families and communities faced with impending changes to their local ecosystems are choosing to adapt to deteriorating environmental conditions by employing a mix of adaptation solutions including redesigning housing structures, adopting new farming techniques or working within family and community units to engage in cyclical labor migration and supporting family

---

[1] R. K. Pachauri, Leo Mayer, and IPCC, eds., *Climate Change 2014: Synthesis Report* (Geneva, Switzerland: Intergovernmental Panel on Climate Change, 2014).
[2] Richard Black et al., "Climate Change: Migration as Adaptation," *Nature* 478 (October 20, 2011): 447–49, https://doi.org/10.1038/478477a.

members and communities through international remittances.

Already, communities around the world are planning and implementing culturally appropriate adaptation and migration strategies that address their own unique needs and aspirations. Many will choose to move well before their homelands become completely uninhabitable and others will choose to not leave at all. Facing a violently changing world marked by catastrophic events set in motion by the actions of people in wealthy industrialized nations, communities at the front lines of the climate crisis are taking direct action to determine their own futures by making plans and employing a mix of adaptation and migration solutions.

While rich industrialized countries are the ones that have created the climate crisis, people in poor and developing regions are likely to weather the most hardship and suffering. Developed countries should not force people experiencing dramatic changes in their local environments to wait until their communities are devastated by floods, droughts, fires and superstorms before opening our borders and communities.

The arbitrary borders and walls separating people and communities around the world are relics of the very capitalist, colonialist system that generated the climate crisis in the first place. Confronting the challenge of climate change requires not only a just transition away from fossil fuels and the preservation of our shared resources, but also opening our borders to welcome all those who want to live, work, learn, and play alongside us.

What Will Climate Migration Look Like?

As the climate continues to change it is clear that some of the places where people are living will become uninhabitable and others will not be able to support current population levels. What is less clear, however, is the scale and scope of this climate change induced migration. Projections range from tens of millions of migrants at the low end to over one billion migrants at the high end with more common projections falling in the range of 150 to 200 million people [3].

There are real and serious political implications for each of these estimates. The higher end estimates are often used by advocates of decisive action on climate change to underscore the severity of the climate crisis and its human impacts. But those same estimates are used by military officials in developed countries to illustrate the security threats created by climate-induced migration. At the other end of the spectrum, lower estimates may undersell the actual human impact of climate change (a family does not need to be forced from their home to experience significant impacts of climate change) while projecting a number of migrants that would be much more feasible for receiving countries to accommodate.

The discrepancies in these predictions can partially be attributed to scientific uncertainty about how different local environments will change as the earth warms, but much more of the uncertainty is derived from the complicated nature of climate-induced migration and the degree to which

---

[3] François Gemenne, "Why the Numbers Don't Add up: A Review of Estimates and Predictions of People Displaced by Environmental Changes," *Global Environmental Change*, Migration and Global Environmental Change – Review of Drivers of Migration, 21 (December 1, 2011): S41–49, https://doi.org/10.1016/j.gloenvcha.2011.09.005.

communities at the front lines of the climate crisis are able to adapt to changing conditions.

To be sure, the climate is changing rapidly but it is not changing overnight. The local effects of climate change are largely slow-onset changes occurring amid a mix of other socio-political transformations. For example, three years of uncommonly severe drought in Syria from 2007 to 2010 caused widespread crop failures and contributed to political instability in the region and ultimately the Syrian civil war [4]. While climate change certainly played a role in setting the stage for the conflict and the resulting refugee crisis, the socio-political choices that world leaders had made in the region had already created a situation where the population was incredibly vulnerable to disruptions of a changing climate.

Even in cases where sea level rise is leaving Pacific Islands literally under water, sea level rise will take time and not everyone will need to (or choose to) leave at the same time. Climate change also may not be the only factors leading people to migrate. [5] In one study, people leaving the Bougainville Island in the Pacific Ocean were asked about their reasons for leaving. Nearly all respondents identified both factors that could be directly related to climate change and factors that predated or had clearly arisen independently of climate change [6].

---

[4] Colin P. Kelley et al., "Climate Change in the Fertile Crescent and Implications of the Recent Syrian Drought," *Proceedings of the National Academy of Sciences of the United States of America* 112, no. 11 (March 17, 2015): 3241–46, https://doi.org/10.1073/pnas.1421533112.
[5] *Outlook on Migration, Environment and Climate Change* (Geneva: International Organization for Migration, 2014).
[6] Johannes Luetz and Peni Hausia Havea, "'We're Not Refugees, We'll Stay Here Until We Die!'—Climate Change Adaptation and Migration Experiences Gathered from the

Throughout human history, communities have faced environmental changes due to natural disasters, droughts, soil erosion and the localized buildup of pollutants. In the case of more modest or incremental changes, the effects have sometimes been requiring no action or limited adaptation measures. As conditions worsen and adaptation becomes increasingly necessary, people's' response mechanisms begin to diverge based on their vulnerability to the effects of these environmental changes and their relative ability to adapt. It is not surprising, then, that faced with the exact same set of environmental changes some people would have the ability stay and take adaptive measures, while other, more vulnerable residents would be forced to leave. And the most vulnerable—those without the resources to migrate—will find themselves trapped.

Choosing to leave home and migrate to another part of the world is perhaps the most consequential decision that a person or family can make, fundamentally altering every aspect of their lives. Environmental drivers are just one of the many factors that may lead people to choose to migrate. Alongside these environmental drivers, social, economic, demographic and political factors all play into individuals' decisions to migrate or their decision to stay [7].

Poor Countries Benefit the Least, Pay the Most

One of the cruelest aspects of anthropogenic climate change is the fact that the communities who are likely to face the most devastating consequences of the warming planet

Tulun and Nissan Atolls of Bougainville, Papua New Guinea," in *Climate Change Impacts and Adaptation Strategies for Coastal Communities*, ed. Walter Leal Filho, Climate Change Management (Cham: Springer International Publishing, 2018), 3–29, https://doi.org/10.1007/978-3-319-70703-7_1.
[7] Black et al., "Climate Change."

are the ones who had the least to do with creating the climate crisis. There is a broad scientific consensus that global climate change is being caused by the buildup of greenhouse gasses in the atmosphere. As these gasses build up, the sun's energy is able to reach the earth's surface but when it is reflected back out, it becomes trapped the way that a greenhouse traps heat keeping plants warm. The most significant greenhouse gas, carbon dioxide a byproduct of burning fossil fuels for energy that has been rapidly accumulating in the atmosphere since the onset of the industrial revolution.

Throughout the nineteenth and twentieth centuries countries in North America and Europe built wealthy industrial economies by burning millions of pounds of fossil fuels to power factories, fuel cars, and trucks, and provide commercial and residential electricity. At the same time, a handful of oil-rich states also amassed enormous wealth by selling crude oil on the world market. More recently emerging economic powers including Brazil, Russia, India, and China have built out their industrial bases joining the list of the top carbon emitters [8].

Today, the wealthy industrialized countries that built their economies by burning fossil fuels and sending millions of pounds of carbon into the atmosphere have the wealth and resources to adapt to the violent effects of climate change by building build seawalls and other infrastructure to protect cities and securing food supplies by purchasing food on the global market. Poorer countries that did not reap the

---

[8] US EPA, "Global Greenhouse Gas Emissions Data," Overviews and Factsheets, US EPA, January 12, 2016, https://www.epa.gov/ghgemissions/global-greenhouse-gas-emissions-data.

economic benefits of the carbon-burning based economy, meanwhile, do not have the resources to fortify their cities to protect against rising sea levels and increasingly violent storms or import food or drinking water as changing weather patterns degrade their farmlands and water supplies.

The people that are most vulnerable to climate change, who will experience the most significant effects and have the most limited abilities to adapt in place or migrate, are those living in the poorest, least developed regions of the world. This experience—living in a world that is rapidly and violently changing because of the callous behaviors of people in rich developed countries—could be understood as the epitome of powerlessness and helplessness. But even in this perfect storm of environmental calamities and indifference, communities on the front lines of the climate crisis are taking direct action to control their futures by making bold, creative, innovative plans to adapt and to migrate in ways that are culturally appropriate and address their own needs and aspirations.

Open Borders—No Apologies and No Compromises

Throughout human history, borders and walls have been used to divide and separate people, communities and cultures. They were created by wars, conquests, processes of colonization, negotiations and treaties. But as the monarch butterfly reminds us as it makes its annual migration from Mexico to Canada, there's nothing natural or permanent about these lines in the ground.

These human-made borders are also not impermeable. The current economic order allows goods and capital to travel back and across borders with almost no meaningful impediments. Business people fly across borders and across oceans to negotiate transactions. Tourists from wealthy countries travel to beach vacations in warmer climates.

The carbon that is emitted from power plants and SUV's in the US, Europe, and the increasingly developed portions of Asia spreads through the atmosphere paying little attention to the lines that humans have drawn on the ground. The changing weather patterns, super storms and droughts brought on by the increase in carbon in the atmosphere spill across borders with no regard to where the carbon was burned or who benefitted.

National borders and walls aren't preventing the movement of money, goods, weather, or wealthy business people and tourists. They are tools to keep poor and working-class people in place and divided. As the climate crisis continues to worsen many people around the world are going to see their local environments change and deteriorate. Many people and many communities will adapt in place, modifying food, energy and water systems and building infrastructure to weather the changing climates. Others will adapt by moving to other parts of the world.

In a world where goods, capital, wealthy people and environmental conditions can move freely, there can be no justifiable excuse for maintaining walls and borders to keep poor and working-class people from moving freely to find the conditions and opportunities to live healthy and fulfilling lives.

Refugees?

Many academics, government agencies, and aid organizations have characterized people participating in climate-induced migration as victims, often advocating for global recognition of climate refugees either under existing refugee protections or a new protocol [9]. While it is clear that climate migrants face a world that is violently and dramatically changing around them—largely as a result of the actions of others—framing climate migrants as victims or refugees presupposes that migration is the only viable response to climate change. This is troubling because it suggests that climate migrants are helpless and without agency. For that reason, many of these climate migrants— people living on or moving from the front lines of the climate crisis—reject the climate refugee frame and these notions of

---

[9] Hedda Ransan-Cooper et al., "Being(s) Framed: The Means and Ends of Framing Environmental Migrants," *Global Environmental Change* 35 (November 2015): 106–15, https://doi.org/10.1016/j.gloenvcha.2015.07.013.

powerlessness[10]. Rather than helpless victims, many climate migrants are courageous survivors, taking direct action to build a better life for themselves and their families in the face of unimaginably challenging circumstances.

Refugees Under International Law

Current international law regarding refugees dates back to the years immediately after the holocaust and World War 2 when the international community established an agreement on the status of refugees of that war and a framework for displaced people going forward. Article 14 of the Universal Declaration of Human Rights of 1948 recognized the right of persons to seek asylum from persecution in other countries. Later the 1951 Convention relating to the Status of Refugees and the 1967 Protocol outlining its application defines a refugee as a person who, *"owing to a well-founded fear of being persecuted for reasons of race, religion, nationality, membership of a particular social group or political opinion is outside of the country of his nationality and is unable or, owing to such fear, is unwilling to avail himself of the protection of that country."* [11]

The 1951 Convention and 1967 Protocol guarantee anyone the right to seek asylum in any signatory country and require that signatory countries either accept those asylum seekers as refugees or facilitate safe passage to a safe third-

---

[10] Luetz and Havea, "'We're Not Refugees, We'll Stay Here Until We Die!'—Climate Change Adaptation and Migration Experiences Gathered from the Tulun and Nissan Atolls of Bougainville, Papua New Guinea"; Karen Elizabeth McNamara and Chris Gibson, "'We Do Not Want to Leave Our Land': Pacific Ambassadors at the United Nations Resist the Category of 'Climate Refugees,'" *Geoforum* 40, no. 3 (May 2009): 475–83, https://doi.org/10.1016/j.geoforum.2009.03.006.
[11] United Nations High Commissioner for Refugees, "Convention and Protocol Relating to the Status of Refugees," UNHCR, accessed January 6, 2019, https://www.unhcr.org/protection/basic/3b66c2aa10/convention-protocol-relating-status-refugees.html.

country willing to accept them as refugees. While asylum seekers not granted refugee status may be relocated to a safe third country, the refugee convention bars signatory countries from returning asylum seekers to a country where they face danger of being persecuted for reasons of race, religion, nationality, membership of a particular social group or political opinion.

Seeking asylum, then, is constructed in international law as a last resort and refugee status is only to be granted to migrants with no other safe alternative. This construction of refugee status necessarily characterizes refugees as helpless and at the mercy of their host country. While this frame is useful in garnering sympathy for climate migrants, it can also rob the people at the front lines of the climate crisis of their agency and autonomy.

There is no requirement under the Convention or Protocol to seek asylum in the first safe country an asylum seeker travels through, nor is there any requirement for asylum seekers to present themselves at a specific port of entry. As a result, central American migrants traveling to the United States through Mexico have an absolute right under international law to seek asylum in the US either at a port of entry or shortly after crossing into the US outside of a port of entry. Further, at this writing (January 2019) the United States does not recognize Mexico as a safe third country so returning central American migrants to Mexico would constitute a violation of the US' obligations under the 1951 Convention.

The situation is slightly different within the European Union. The Dublin Protocol requires asylum seekers arriving in the EU to request asylum and be fingerprinted in the first EU country they arrive in and that their asylum claim be processed there.

This system has forced much of the burden of the current refugee crisis on EU border states and acted to shield some of the wealthier EU states from increases in migration.

Notably, international law regarding refugees and asylum seekers only applies to people who are forced to cross national borders. People who are forced from their homes but are able to migrate within the borders of their home countries are categorized as internally displaced people (IDPs). Internally displaced people are granted some protections under the UN's Guiding Principles on Internal Displacement and often some support from the UN High Commission on Refugees, but generally speaking, the wellbeing and treatment of internally displaced people is considered to be within the prevue of national authorities.

A New Paradigm in Climate Migration

Although climate-induced migration bears many similarities to other historical modes of migration, the climate crisis presents the world with a brand-new frame for international migration. Where historic flows of migration could be ebbed by addressing the factors leading to displacement—ending violent conflicts, improving local economic conditions or offering protections to persecuted populations—the time when climate change could be completely prevented has long passed. While serious action to reduce emissions of greenhouse gasses is necessary and can likely ameliorate some of the most devastating consequences of climate change, environmental conditions around the world are rapidly changing and no amount of political posturing or climate change denial is going to change that.

Further, many of the worst effects of climate change are fully anticipatable. It may be difficult to predict where war, famine or economic depression will lead to mass displacement, but current climate change models offer some reliable predictions about areas of the world that are likely to become uninhabitable. As sea levels rise large swaths of land will find themselves underwater, as temperatures rise some arable farmland will become less viable, and as glaciers melt regions will see their rivers dry and lose key sources of potable water.

The predictable nature of climate change allows for communities on the front lines of the climate crisis to make plans to adapt or migrate before conditions actually deteriorate. While waves of mass migration are often reactive—people fleeing war, natural disaster, or famine—climate induced migration can be anticipatory. By making plans and beginning to migrate *before* disaster sets in, people on the front lines of the climate crisis can reduce the human and financial costs of being forced to flee their homes.

Anticipatory climate migration, however, demands a new paradigm for international migration. Current international law only offers refugee protection to people who can no longer stay in their home countries (and then only if their displacement is caused by persecution based on race, religion, nationality, membership of a particular social group or political opinion). Public and political support for humanitarian aid for people displaced by disasters is strong. In the aftermath of Typhoon Haiyan, the international community raised more than $300 million in aid, and after Hurricane Mitch battered much of Central America the US government offered Temporary Protected Status for migrants from Honduras and Nicaragua. But to date, there have been no similar mobilizations of support for people leaving their homes in anticipation of climate change.

The reactive nature of traditional responses to humanitarian crises assures a worst-case scenario for people forced from their homes by changes in their climate. Without viable options for planned migration in anticipation of changes in the climate, people on the front lines of the climate crisis are forced to wait until disaster strikes before receiving aid or legal immigration status on dry ground.

Forcing communities to wait for conditions to deteriorate to the point that storms, floods and other acute events forces residents to evacuate often leads to people leaving their homes and possessions behind, without time to make plans for their travel or destination [12]. The consequences of waiting for disaster strike can be devastating.

It is telling that the cautionary tale about not preparing for climate change that is cited again and again in the literature on climate migration is not a small island in the Pacific Ocean. Rather, it is an industrialized city that is home to two oil refineries and at the time did not teach climate change as a fact in its public schools: New Orleans. When Hurricane Katrina hit New Orleans, more than a million people were forced from their homes with 600,000 still displaced months later; damages climbed to $150 billion, and at least

---

[12] Todd Edward William Schenk, "Finding the Higher Ground: Assessing Contrasting Approaches to Planning for Climate Change Induced Resettlement" (Thesis, Massachusetts Institute of Technology, 2009), http://dspace.mit.edu/handle/1721.1/50123.

986 people were killed. Forty-percent of those killed in the storm drowned in the flooding [13].

In New Orleans, policymakers had the hubris to deny that climate change was even happening and they refused to make serious adaptation plans. And when it was clear that a major storm was coming, the evacuation plan left the most vulnerable—poor Black residents who could not afford to load up their SUV and drive north for a few days—behind to die in the flood.

Beyond the human and financial costs of failing to take steps to adapt to the changing climate, preventing people from migrating before conditions deteriorate create serious political instability, fueling conflict and leaving behind a string of failed states. As early as 2004, US military leaders recognized the military and security risks of unaddressed climate change, commissioning the study, "An Abrupt Climate Change Scenario and Its Implications for the United States." Later, in 2008 Congress mandated that the national-security impacts of climate change be included the Department of Defense Quadrennial Defense Review. Climate change is now widely recognized by security experts as a threat multiplier for instability because of its potential to generate resource scarcity, conflict over those scarce resources and mass migration[14].

With the benefit of projections about the most severe impacts of climate change, people living on the front lines of the climate crisis are taking action to avoid some of the most

---

[13] Allison Plyer, "Facts for Features: Katrina Impact," The Data Center, August 26, 2016, https://www.datacenterresearch.org/data-resources/katrina/facts-for-impact/.
[14] Christian Parenti, *Tropic of Chaos: Climate Change and the New Geography of Violence* (New York: Nation Books, 2011).

disastrous consequences of climate change imaged in these security assessments. In many cases, populations vulnerable to the effects of climate change are implementing adaptation measures to allow them to stay in their homes— or at least in their home countries. In other cases, comprehensive and early preparation are ensuring a best-case-scenario for planned migration, ensuring that migrants have the best-available knowledge about the risks and opportunities and are able to make choices that are appropriate for themselves and for their communities[15].

In order for people to effectively plan and adapt to the changing climates we must remove the artificial boundaries preventing people from moving. We need to open borders around the world to allow people and communities on the front lines of the climate crisis to identify and actualize long-term, culturally appropriate strategies to adapt to the changing global climate.

---

[15] "Planned Relocation, Disasters and Climate Change: Consolidating Good Practices and Preparing for the Future" (UNHCR, March 2014), http://www.unhcr.org/54082cc69.pdf.

Communities on the Front Lines Facing Down the Climate Crisis

Migration with Dignity in Kiribati

Kiribati is a low-lying atoll island in the central Pacific Ocean, located 8,000 km northeast of Australia and 5,500 km northeast of New Zealand with a population of around 100,000. With most of the nation's islands rising less than 3 meters above sea level with widths spanning just a few hundred meters, Kiribati is particularly vulnerable to rising sea levels. In anticipation of global climate change drowning a large portion of the nation's landmass and rendering other areas uninhabitable because of soil erosion and salinization of water tables, the Kiribati government has established a complex, multi-modal response to climate change.

Starting in 2003, Kiribati launched the Kiribati Adaptation Program (KAP) to reduce the nation's vulnerability to climate change. The program aims to improve water supply management, employ coastal management protection measures such as mangrove replanting efforts, reduce coastal erosion and, most notably, facilitate population resettlement planning to reduce personal risks.[16]

Recognizing that even if some of the island nation's land remains above ground agricultural prospects will become increasingly limited, the Kiribati government has looked

---

[16] "Kiribati Adaptation Program | Climate Change," accessed December 8, 2018, http://www.climate.gov.ki/category/action/adaptation/kiribati-adaptation-program/.

abroad for sources of food security. In 2014 Kiribati completed the purchase of a 5,460-acre tract of farmland in Fiji for $9.3 million. Since the purchase of the land people in both Kiribati and Fiji have predicted that the government intended to relocate Kiribati residents to the land, but the government has insisted that the land is to be used only for agricultural production[17].

Even with the most robust adaptation measures, current trends in sea level rise dictate that at some point in the not-too-distant future, a significant portion of Kiribati's population will need to leave the atoll nation. Recognizing that a failure to plan for a slow, methodical and dignified migration, departure would likely look more like an evacuation than a migration, the Kiribati government has implemented a long-term planned migration program to ensure I-Kiribati the right to "migrate with dignity."

The "migration with dignity" policy is a two-pronged approach providing opportunities for citizens who want to migrate abroad now (or in the near future) and as well as those who will move over the longer term, offer educational and vocational training to ensure that I-Kiribati expatriates are able to find work in receiving countries. In the near term, Kiribati is working to forge expatriate communities and social networks in various receiving countries who will be able to support future migrants and send back remittances to

---

[17] Elfriede Hermann and Wolfgang Kempf, "Climate Change and the Imagining of Migration: Emerging Discourses on Kiribati's Land Purchase in Fiji," *Contemporary Pacific; Honolulu* 29, no. 2 (2017): 231-263,404-405, https://search.proquest.com/docview/1924251690/abstract/77E035547E7149D5PQ/1.

support those staying behind as the country's economy shrinks[18].

These ex-patriot communities will also help to preserve Kiribati's unique history and culture within the diaspora. In an interview with The Wire, Claire Anterea, the founder of the Kiribati Climate Action Network International, expressed that I-Kiribati, young and old, are concerned about losing their traditions, noting "our culture [is] an oral culture that is shared from generation to generation. And therefore, our local knowledge is passed on from generation to generation by word of mouth. The challenge for preserving [it] will not be easy" [19].

Over the longer term, Kiribati is working with host countries to develop educational and vocational programs to train I-Kiribati migrants in skills that are in high demand on the global market. The Kiribati-Australia Nursing Initiative (KANI) offers migrants training in nursing, complete with Australian nursing certifications. Other programs promote labor migration in the agricultural, hospitality, seafaring industries [20].

Not everyone in Kiribati is excited about moving, however. The Kiribati government has been clear that 'relocation will always be viewed as an option of last resort' and 26% of Kiribati indicate that they are not willing to move to another country, even in the long term [21]. Some of those

---

[18] Karen McNamara, "Cross-Border Migration with Dignity in Kiribati," Forced Migration Review, May 2015, https://www.fmreview.org/climatechange-disasters/mcnamara.
[19] Kayla Walsh, "Kiribati Prepares for 'Migration With Dignity' to Confront the Ravages of Climate Change," The Wire, July 15, 2017, https://thewire.in/culture/kiribati-migration-climate-change.
[20] Walsh; Kelly Wyett, "Escaping a Rising Tide: Sea Level Rise and Migration in Kiribati," Asia & the Pacific Policy Studies 1, no. 1 (January 1, 2014): 171–85, https://doi.org/10.1002/app5.7.
[21] Wyett, "Escaping a Rising Tide."

more reluctant to embrace relocation include religious and traditional leaders who cite the I-Kiribati's strong ties to their lands.

Even those who stay behind can reap some of the benefits of out-migration. Migration can alleviate pressures on the resource base and remittances can provide important sources of income for those who stay behind. For their part, those who stay behind can help the diaspora continue to maintain their history and culture and connection to their traditional homelands.

Newtok Village in Alaska Moves to Higher Ground

Newtok is a Yup'ik Eskimo village of around 400 residents along the Niglick River in western Alaska. Up until the late 19th century ancestors of the Newtok maintained a migratory lifestyle, moving seasonally among coastal and inland hunting and fishing camps but by the beginning of the 20th century the US Department of the Interior's Bureau of Education build schools in the region and required Alaska Native children to attend them. The compulsory education system forced the Alaska Native population to abandon their traditional practices and settle in small, permanent villages [22].

By the early 1980s environmental conditions in the village began to deteriorate as melting permafrost accelerated erosion, pushing the Niglick River closer and closer to the village. The State of Alaska spent about $1.5 million to control erosion before 1990 but the continued thaw of the permafrost

---

[22] Robin Bronen and F. Stuart Chapin, "Adaptive Governance and Institutional Strategies for Climate-Induced Community Relocations in Alaska," *Proceedings of the National Academy of Sciences* 110, no. 23 (June 4, 2013): 9320–25, https://doi.org/10.1073/pnas.1210508110.

only accelerated the erosion and the river continued to creep closer and closer to the village.

By 1994, residents of the Newtok village voted to move to higher ground, but at the time there was no clear location to resettle and no resources to facilitate the move. By 2003 the village secured a new site just a few miles away on Nelson Island in a land trade with the US Fish and Wildlife Service, but the new site had no infrastructure and there was no apparent funding source for such an ambitious project. In 2006 an ad-hoc intergovernmental working group led by the Newtok Traditional Council, called the Newtok Planning Group, was formed and initiated a strategic relocation process [23].

As one of the first, but unfortunately certainly not the last, communities in the US to be forced to resettle because of the changing climate, the experience of the Netwok village illustrated a major gap in federal planning and emergency management laws. While millions of dollars could be quickly deployed to respond to a sudden onset disaster, current funding mechanisms simply had not contemplated a situation like the one the Newtok were experiencing. For years the Newtok cobbled together a piecemeal of funding from different federal agencies to start work on new houses, a barge landing, and other infrastructure this all fell short of the capital needed to begin relocation in earnest [24].

---

[23] Robin Bronen, "Climate-Induced Displacement of Alaska Native Communities," Alaska Immigration Justice Project (Brookings Institute, January 30, 2013), https://www.brookings.edu/wp-content/uploads/2016/06/30-climate-alaska-bronen-paper.pdf.
[24] Rachel Waldholz, "Newtok Asks: Can the U.S. Deal with Slow-Motion Climate Disasters?" *KTOO Public Media* (blog), January 6, 2017, https://www.ktoo.org/2017/01/06/newtok-asks-can-u-s-deal-slow-motion-climate-disasters/.

Then in March of 2018, more than twenty years after the villagers first voted to move, Congress allocated an extra $15 million to the federal Denali Commission in the federal budget to jump-start the move. While the one-time allotment falls far short of the total price tag of around $100 million needed to facilitate the entire move, it will allow the community to move forward. Relocation coordinators anticipate residents living in the new village on a full-time basis by fall of 2019 [25].

At first glance, $100 million, or even the $15 million allotted to jumpstart the project, seems like a staggering sum to fund the relocation of a village of 400, but in reality that number is only a fraction of the cost of waiting for disaster to hit instead of engaging in planned migration. In 2005, Hurricane Katrina displaced more than 1 million residents, resulting in more than 986 deaths and costing $150 billion in damages and $75 billion in emergency relief [26]. The per-capita financial cost of Hurricane Katrina was $225,000 while the per capita cost of providing the seed money to relocate the Newtok village was just $37,500 and not a single Newtok village was killed in the process.

In light of the incredibly high costs of disaster relief and the comparatively low costs of relocation, providing financial support to communities that want to move is a surprisingly cost-effective method of adapting to climate change. More importantly, in this case, planned migration allowed the Newtok village to stay intact, maintaining their cultural identity and history—something that should be considered a

---

[25] Rachel Waldholz, "Newtok to Congress: Thank You for Saving Our Village," *Alaska Public Media*, March 27, 2018, https://www.alaskapublic.org/2018/03/27/newtok-to-congress-thank-you-for-saving-our-village/.
[26] Plyer, "Facts for Features: Katrina Impact."

welcomed disruption to the US government's 500-years-long program of erasing indigenous cultures on this continent.

The Newtok is not the only Alaska Native village exploring relocation in the face of the brutal effects of climate change. Currently, three other Alaskan communities, the Shishmaref, Kivalina, and Shaktoolik communities have made the decision to relocate. None of these three communities, however, have the type of concrete plans developed by the Netwok for their relocation, nor have they secured financing to facilitate the move [27].

Climate Migration in Vietnam

Vietnam is the world's fifteenth most populous country with a total population of around 95 million and also one of the countries most susceptible to rising sea levels. Research by the World Bank predicts that 10.8% of Vietnam's population would be impacted by a 1-meter rise in sea levels and 35% of the population would be impacted by a 5-meter rise in sea levels. Notably, the majority of the impact would occur in the agriculturally and industrial important areas in the Mekong and Red River Deltas [28]. In addition to potentially overtaking land mass, rising sea levels are also likely to force seawater into deltas, salinating water supplies used for drinking and irrigation.

While Vietnam has developed a commercial and industrial base in recent years, it is only responsible for 0.57% of global carbon emissions or just 2.2 tons per capita, making

---

[27] Bronen, "Climate-Induced Displacement of Alaska Native Communities."
[28] Susmita Dasgupta et al., "The Impact of Sea Level Rise on Developing Countries: A Comparative Analysis," February 2007, 51.

it one of the world's smallest emitters of CO2 and one of the countries least culpable in the climate crisis [29].

In recent years, climate change has fueled a wave of internal migration in Vietnam. Between 2010 and 2015 13.6% of Vietnam's population migrated internally[30]. A large portion of this migration has involved people moving away from flooding agricultural areas. Over the past 10 years the population of the Mekong Delta, one of the world's most productive agricultural regions, has dropped by an astonishing 1 million, with 14.5% of migrants citing climate change as the dominant factor in their decision [31].

While the vast majority of migration decisions are individual and family decisions, the Vietnamese government has implemented an impressive framework to support planned internal migration as climate change renders areas increasingly uninhabitable. As part of the 2008 National Target Program to Respond to Climate Change, the government of Vietnam implemented a program offering substantial support for households that needing to relocate. The program offered $880-$1,100 USD per household for relocation expenses, land allotments, 12 months of food, and vocational training and credit from the Social Policy Bank. In many cases, families moving to higher ground retained

---

[29] "World Development Indicators - Google Public Data Explorer," accessed December 8, 2018,
https://www.google.com/publicdata/explore?ds=d5bncppjof8f9_&ctype=l&strail=false&nselm=h&met_y=en_atm_co2e_kt&dl=en.

[30] Thampitakkull Jakkree, "Overview of Internal Migration in Viet Nam," *UNESCO Bangkok*, February 2018, 9.

[31] Alex Chapman and Van Pham Dang Tri, "Climate Change Is Triggering a Migrant Crisis in Vietnam," The Conversation, January 9, 2018,
http://theconversation.com/climate-change-is-triggering-a-migrant-crisis-in-vietnam-88791.

ownership of their own land to continue farming until it became unviable.

Notably, the relocation aspect of the 2008 NTP and later relocation programs did not simply act to move people out of flooding lands. Relocations under the NTP were also explicitly linked to the National Target Program on New Rural Development (NTPNRD), an existing program focusing on rural development and poverty reduction, ensuring that relocation sites offer access to electricity, water, health and education services, and public roads [32].

Interestingly, although climate change is already leading to deteriorating conditions in parts of the country, in recent years international emigration from Vietnam has been relatively modest with only about 2.9% of the population living abroad [33]. Vietnam's strategy of implementing planned internal relocation programs in concert with existing programs aimed at reducing rural poverty provides an interesting model for facilitating climate-induced migration, allowing migrants to stay as close as possible to their homes while also improving their standard of living. It is not clear, however, whether this level of internal migration will remain sustainable indefinitely or if Vietnam is likely to reach a tipping point when rural resettlement areas and cities become overwhelmed with internal migrants from cities.

---

[32] "Planned Relocation for Communities in the Context of Environmental Change and Climate Change - A Training Manual for Provincial and Local Authorities" (International Organization for Migration, December 2017), https://environmentalmigration.iom.int/sites/default/files/training_manual_on_planned_relocation_eng.pdf.
[33] Jakkree, "Overview of Internal Migration in Viet Nam."

Climate Changes Fuels Migration from the Northern Triangle

In fall of 2018 a caravan of migrants fleeing violence in the Northern Triangle of Central America (El Salvador, Guatemala, and Honduras) to seek asylum in the United States brought light to an international humanitarian crisis playing out through central America. Individuals and families participating in the caravan identified a complex set of factors leading to their decision to move—ranging from endemic poverty, to plans to reunite with their families in the United States, but the dominant factor migrants cited as pushing them north was the epidemic of gang violence throughout the region.

While the reasons that individuals choose to migrate are complex and the epidemic of gang violence has undeniably played the defining role in forcing people to migrate, it is also clear that the changing climate played an important role in creating the conditions that led to the deteriorating political and economic situation in the Northern Triangle. In Honduras where 14% of the economy is reliant on agriculture, farmers faced major droughts in 2017 and 2018 and the average temperature has already increased over 1-degree Fahrenheit in the last decade. In El Salvador 21% of the population work in the country's imperiled agricultural sector and the country's rivers are rapidly drying up.[34]

In the coming years, climate change is only likely to worsen conditions in the Northern Triangle. By 2050, production of the region's key cash crop, coffee, is expected

---

[34] 'The Caravan Is a Climate Change Story', *Sierra Club*, 2018 <https://www.sierraclub.org/sierra/root-migration-climate-change-caravan-central-america> [accessed 2 March 2019].

to decline by 40%.[35] To be certain, the reasons that people are making the dangerous journey north to seek asylum in the United States are myriad and complex. But for years, the changing climate added fuel to the economic and political challenges facing the region.

Migrant caravans moving north are just one part of the story of migration as adaptation to climate change the Northern Triangle. Once in the United States, migrants often send remittances back to their families to provide for basic needs and, in some cases, invest in local development projects. Indeed, remittances account for a significant portion of GDP in El Salvador, Guatemala and Honduras.

---

[35] 'The Caravan Is a Climate Change Story'.

Front Line Solutions for Global Challenges

The world's climate is rapidly and violently changing in ways that are likely to make significant areas where people are currently living completely uninhabitable and dramatically reducing the populations that other areas can accommodate. While there are real and meaningful things that developed nations can and should be doing right now to dramatically reduce emissions of greenhouse gasses to dampen the effects of the climate change, poor communities on the front lines of the climate crisis are already facing an overwhelming onslaught of superstorms, floods, droughts, and rising sea levels.

Anthropogenic climate change is truly a global challenge that will require global action, particularly from the countries most culpable in generating the climate crisis. In 2010, in the aftermath of the failed climate talks in Copenhagen during the 15th UN Conference of the Parties, representatives from developing countries around the world and thousands of civil society organizations gathered in Cochabamba, Bolivia for the World People's Conference on Climate Change and the Rights of Mother Earth to develop the Peoples Agreement platform demanding that developing countries take dramatic action to reduce carbon emissions, eliminate restrictive immigration policies to offer a decent life to people forced to migrate due to climate change, and create an adaptation fund to compensate developing countries for current and future damages and support local adaptation measures [36].

In the 2015 Paris Climate Agreement, developed countries agreed to set a goal of contributing a combined $100 billion dollars per year to support developing countries in sustainable development, climate change mitigation and adaptation. The agreement fell short, however, on offering any sort of protection for climate migrants, sidestepping the issue by developing a task force to develop recommendations on displacement [37]. In the following years, however, even the modest steps forward agreed upon in the Paris Agreement were eroded as the US withdrew from the agreement and developed countries fell short on their financial commitments, even after attempting to game the rules of the agreement by including loans and non-climate related contributions towards the $100 billion target [38].

While the developed countries who are responsible for the climate crisis certainly have a role in financing climate change mitigation and adaptation, decisions about how to implement adaptation measures must be left to the people who are directly impacted. In one particularly egregious financing mechanism, the reducing emissions from deforestation and forest degradation (REDD+) developed countries are allowed to 'offset' their own carbon emissions by 'paying' developing forest-rich countries to preserve their forest lands. These payments, then, entitle developed

---

[36] "Peoples Agreement," *World People's Conference on Climate Change and the Rights of Mother Earth* (blog), January 5, 2010, https://pwccc.wordpress.com/support/.
[37] UNFCCC, "The Paris Agreement," 2015, 31.
[38] Sabrina Shankman, "Wealthy Countries Accused of Trying to Weaken Paris Climate Finance Rules," InsideClimate News, September 10, 2018, https://insideclimatenews.org/news/10092018/paris-climate-negotiations-bangkok-rulebook-climate-finance-developing-countries-china-trump.

countries to dictate how forests are to be preserved, which has generally translated to forcing forest-dependent indigenous people from their lands to make way for externally-imposed forestry practices [39].

In the face of a rising tides of climate change people around the world are facing down the climate crisis, bracing for the blow, making plans and taking action to adapt to the changing world. By doing so they are not just finding solutions to an impending crisis, they are reclaiming control over their own future. The I-Kiribati are deploying a sophisticated program to maintain their identity, culture, and history as they prepare to put themselves for employment overseas. But the I-Kiribati's futures are not dictated for them, it will be up to each family and individual to decide on the future that matches with their abilities, needs, and aspirations. It was not some outside force that decided that the Netwok village would be moved, the villagers voted to move—four times— and they worked tirelessly to devise a feasible relocation strategy and demand the resources they needed to move. By embracing their ancestors' migratory traditions and moving to higher ground, Newtok villagers are disrupting a 500-year history of erasing native cultures. As the delta regions of Vietnam flood and are threatened by increasing salinization Vietnamese farmers are moving to higher ground, creating even more resilient conditions than before and reducing rates of rural poverty.

To be certain, the climate crisis is causing a violent disruption to the lives of people living on the front lines. But by

---

[39] Joanna Cabello and Tamra Gilbertson, "A Colonial Mechanism to Enclose Lands: A Critical Review of Two REDD+-Focused Special Issues," *Ephemera, Theory & Politics in Organization*, 2012, http://www.ephemerajournal.org/sites/default/files/12-1cabellogilbertson.pdf.

recognizing the coming threat and having the courage, creativity, and imagination to develop bold plans to move entire villages or reorganize an agricultural production in one of the world's most populous countries, people on the front lines of the climate crisis are staring down the rising tides and creating better futures for themselves and their families.

While the specific adaptation and migration programs adopted by communities that have already been forced to respond to changing climates may not be immediately transferable to the innumerable other communities that will face dramatically changing environmental conditions in the coming decades, some commonalities are instructive. In each case, plans were developed and implemented by the countries and the people who would ultimately live through these changes, not by an outside force. Although the brunt of the cost and the pain of relocating and adapting was born by the communities themselves, financial support from industrialized nations has played an important role in facilitating the implementation of the plans. Additionally, while national or community-level planning has created options for migration and adaptation in the case of Kiribati and Vietnam, individuals and their families were able to exercise autonomy in finding the most appropriate solution for their individual circumstances. In the case of the much smaller Netwok village, the wholesale relocation a village, the move was the result of a clear and overwhelming will of the entire village following four affirmative votes and years of self-advocacy for the move.

As the climate crisis deepens, we can expect more and more communities around the world to be faced with dramatic changes to their local environments. As the experience in the Gulf Coast in the aftermath of Hurricane Katrina reminds us, waiting until disaster hits to adapt can be incredibly costly, in both money and human life. In the face of immeasurable challenges, people around the world are asserting agency and developing people-driven dynamic plans for adaptation and migration that meet the needs and the aspirations of their communities.

Industrialized nations can play an important role in supporting this adaptation by heeding the demands of people from around the developing world laid out in the People's Agreement: taking aggressive action to slow the crisis and lessen the blow of climate change by cutting carbon emissions dramatically and immediately, eliminating barriers to migration for people impacted by the climate crisis, and providing funding to support the adaptation and migration efforts of people living on the front lines of the climate crisis. But the brilliant work of the people in Kiribati, the Newtok Village, and Vietnam show that developing powerful and creative strategies for climate adaptation and migration can—and should—be led by the communities that are on the front lines of the climate crisis.

Get Involved with Rising Tide North America

Get connected with the climate justice movement and get support for your work.

Rising Tide North America (RTNA) is a network of radical climate justice groups and individuals across North America working to confront the root causes of climate change. Get plugged into the RTNA Network to connect with other climate and environmental justice organizers and get valuable support for your work.

Get the Word Out About Your Work!

Let us know about your actions and activities and we can help to spread the word. Almost 7,000 people are following @RisingTideNA on Twitter and more than 15,000 people 'like' us on Facebook. We also maintain a high-traffic website, www.RisingTideNorthAmerica.org and an e-mail list with 16,000 subscribers. If you want us to promote your group's work on online, tweet at us, message us on Facebook, or e-mail us at communications@RisingTideNorthAmerica.org.

Get the Resources You Need!

The RTNA Action Fund has limited funding to give grants to grassroots groups working to defend their communities and their environment from fossil fuel extraction. Grants usually do not exceed $500, however in urgent situations groups can receive up to $1,000. For more details or to apply visit www.risingtidenorthamerica.org/actionfund/

Get Connected with Other Climate Justice Organizers

RTNA creates intentional spaces for network groups and allies to connect to build relationships, strategize, and support each other's work. We maintain a low-traffic e-mail list serve for local contacts, host quarterly conference calls on timely developments in our movement. RTNA also coordinates regional networks bringing together local groups facing similar issues in different regions around North America. To get plugged into the network and connect with other climate justice organizers contact local@RisingTideNorthAmerica.org.

Get Trained Up!

The RTNA Trainers Network can get you in touch with skilled trainers who can help you and your local group build the skills you need to fight climate change! The trainers network offers trainings in action planning, strategy, organizing skills, media work, and tactical skills. Find out more about the trainers network or get in touch with a trainer in your area at trainers.RisingTideNorthAmerica.org or e-mail us at trainers@RisingTideNorthAmerica.org.

Share Ideas About What It Takes to Win!

Rising Tide groups and organizers around the continent are employing new and innovative strategies and tactics to confront the root causes of climate change. The Rising Tide Network's 'Creative Collaborations' working group brings together organizers to create radical analysis on our work and the climate crisis. Rising Tide has put together publications such as 'Hoodwinked in the Hot House,' 'Making Green a

Threat Again,' and helped to promote and circulate movement analysis pieces written by Rising Tide activists like "The Climate Movement's Keystone Preoccupation." If you have an idea for a publication or you want to join the conversation about what it takes to win, e-mail the analysis@RisingTideNorthAmerica.org.